NATIONAL GEOGRAPHIC KiDS

IN MY BACKYARD

STICKER ACTIVITY BOOK

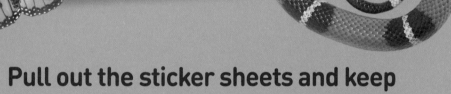

Pull out the sticker sheets and keep them by you as you complete each page. There are also lots of extra stickers to use in this book or anywhere you want! Have fun!

NATIONAL GEOGRAPHIC
Washington, D.C.

Consultant: Richard Walker
Editorial, Design, and Production by
make believe ideas

Picture credits: All images Shutterstock unless noted as follows:
Corbis: 26 tl (mole), Gerry Ellis/NGS: 29 tr (fox squirrel), **Matt Propert/NGS:** 18 m (hooded oriole),
Alex Snyder/NGS: 18 br (northern cardinal), 28 br (chipmunk), 29 bl (chipmunk),
Make Believe Ideas: 1 tr (tortoise); mr (snake), 4 bl (maple leaf), 6 tl (children x 3), 14 tr, 25 m (logs),
33 tr (coral snake); mr (California kingsnake); tm; mr (corn snake), 38 m (flower), 40 bl (snail).

Sticker pages: All images **Shutterstock** unless noted as follows:
Alex Snyder/NGS: 18, 19 Carolina wren, 28, 29 chipmunk hexagon,
Make Believe Ideas: 4, 5 squirrel, Extra Stickers (Sheet 1) tortoise, 6, 7 ball; drum; pinwheel;
skittles; train, Extra Stickers (Sheet 2) butterfly; snail, 12, 13 green scarab beetle,
Extra Stickers (Sheet 5) tortoise, Extra Stickers (Sheet 8) milksnake, **NGS:** 2, 3 hose, trowel.

Printed in China. 21/MBI/3

How does your garden grow?

Most plants need sun, warmth, water, and food from the soil to grow.

Sticker the things this plant needs to grow, then add color.

How many ladybugs can you count?

5

You can grow food in vegetable patches, but some animals might eat your plants!

Sticker the tools in the shed.

rabbit

turtle

snail

Count how many of each animal you can find in the vegetable patch.

3

Some trees lose their leaves in winter.

You can use a tree's leaves to tell what kind of tree it is!

oak leaf

maple leaf

Sticker and color the leaves.

orange tree leaf

willow leaf

Trees that lose their leaves once a year are called deciduous. Can you say de-sid-you-us?

Do you have a favorite type of tree? Draw it here!

Some animals live in trees!

Color and sticker the animals around the tree.

5

Backyards can be lots of fun!

You can turn your backyard into a cool playground with a tree house and toys!

Follow the lines to see which child gets to the tree house.

Color the jungle gym.

How many chipmunks can you count?

Sticker more toys!

Butterflies can have bright wings.

Like all insects, butterflies have six legs and a body made of three parts.

Draw lines to match the pairs of butterflies.

Use stickers to finish the butterfly's wing.

Find the missing stickers.

monarch

California sister

red admiral

purple admiral

western tiger swallowtail

orange sulphur

9

Some bees make honey.

Honeybees create honey and store it in their hives.

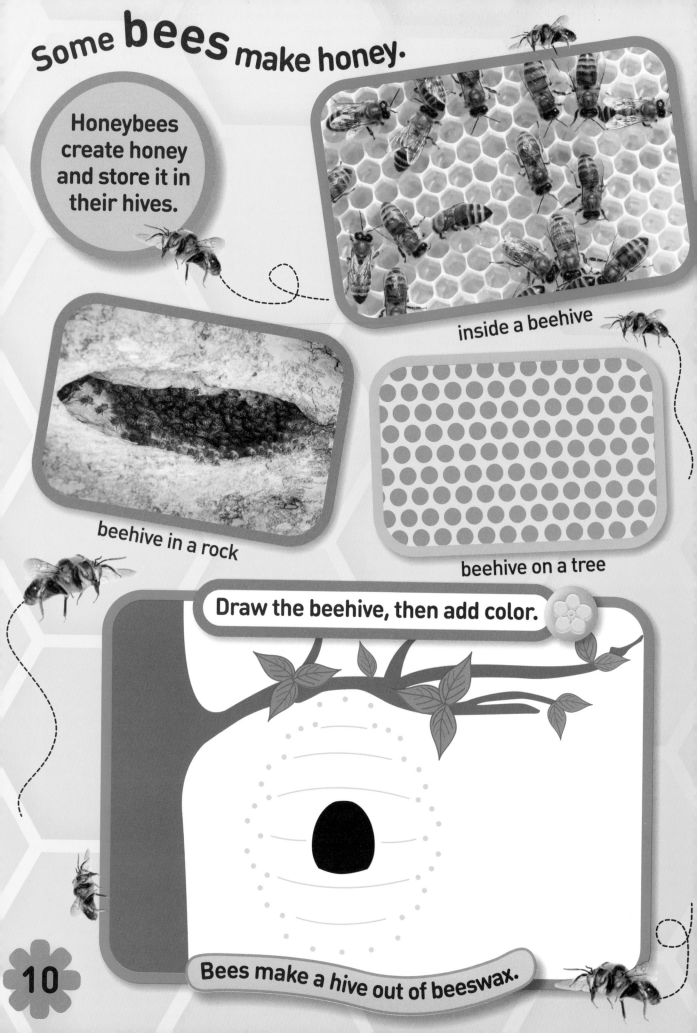

inside a beehive

beehive in a rock

beehive on a tree

Draw the beehive, then add color.

Bees make a hive out of beeswax.

Bees can be many different colors. They can be green, black and white, and even blue!

blue carpenter bee

sweat bee

Find the bee that's different.

Beetles have hard wings.

Beetles are insects with hard outer wings that look like shells.

rhinoceros beetle

Colorado potato beetle

Japanese beetle

snout beetle

Find the missing stickers.

Dung beetles can push up to 50 times their weight in poop!

Color the beetles.

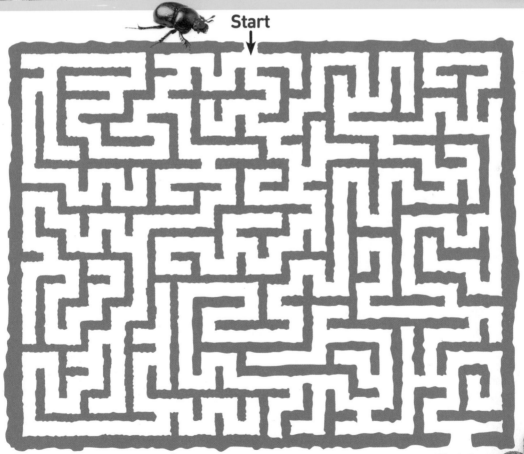

Start

Finish

Help the dung beetle find its way to the dung.

Bugs can be fast and slow!

Slugs and snails are part of a group of animals called gastropods.

⭐ Sticker shells on the snails.

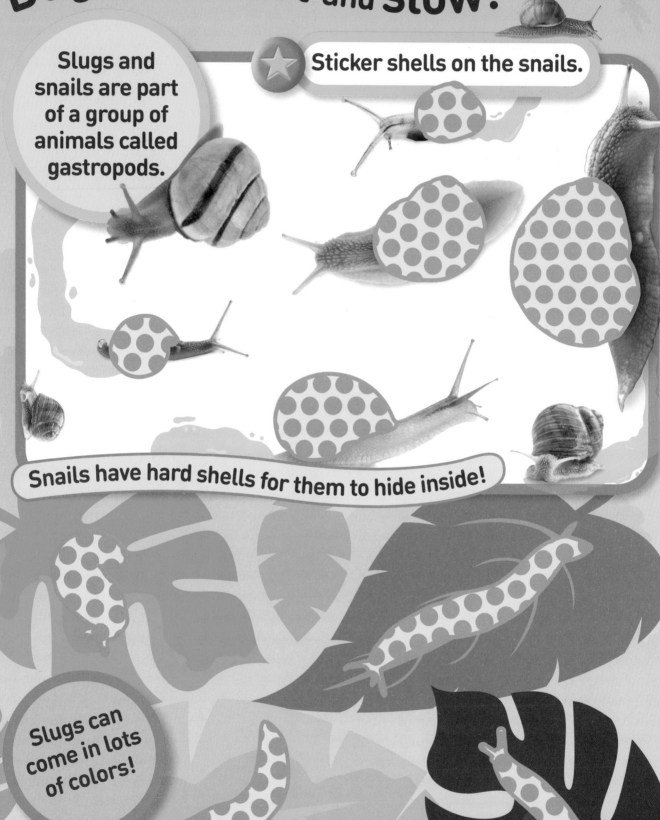

Snails have hard shells for them to hide inside!

Slugs can come in lots of colors!

Find the colorful slug stickers, then stick them on the matching leaves.

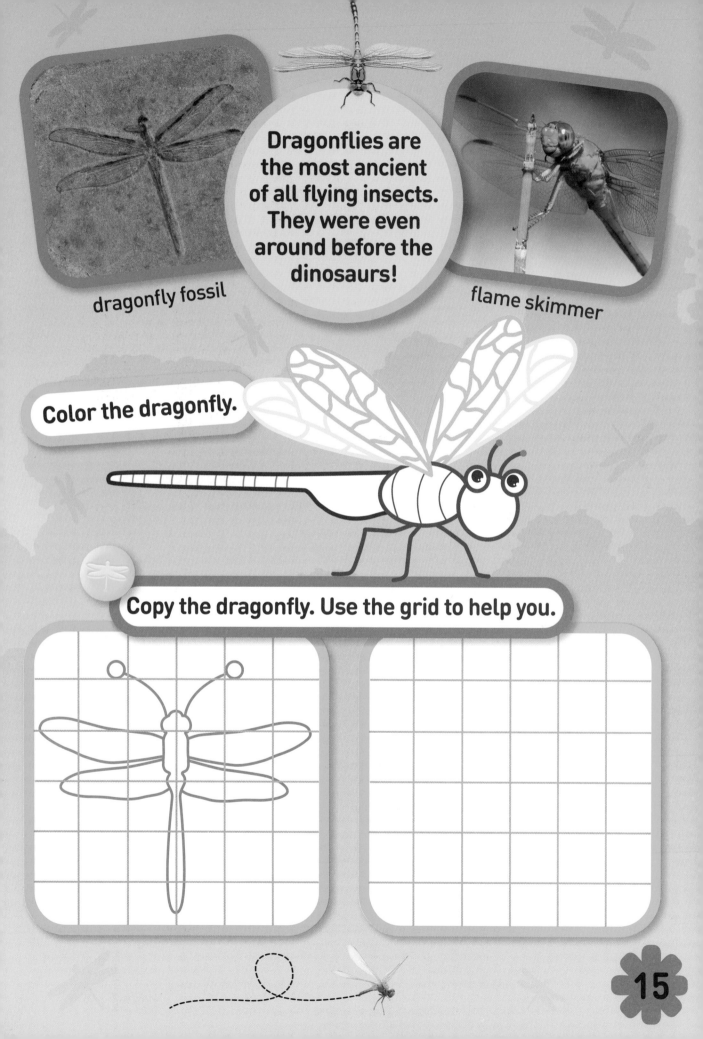

dragonfly fossil

Dragonflies are the most ancient of all flying insects. They were even around before the dinosaurs!

flame skimmer

Color the dragonfly.

Copy the dragonfly. Use the grid to help you.

Some **spiders** spin **webs.**

Some spiders use silk to make webs, some use it to climb, and some spiders use their silk as a parachute!

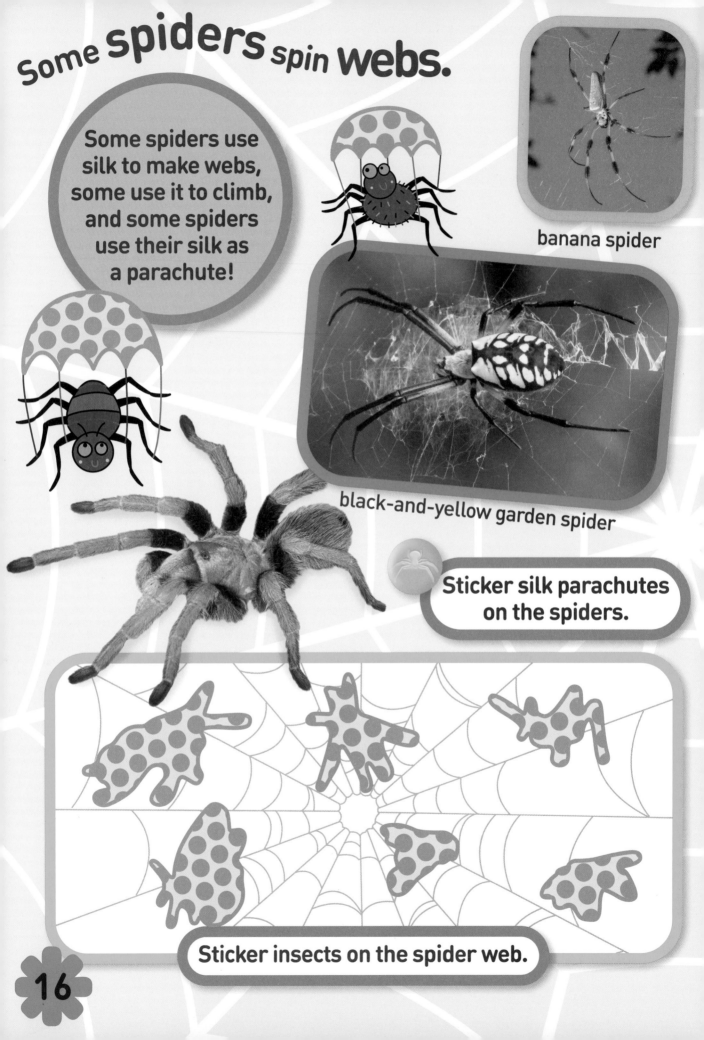

banana spider

black-and-yellow garden spider

Sticker silk parachutes on the spiders.

Sticker insects on the spider web.

16

Mexican red-kneed
tarantula

A tarantula's
venom is less
poisonous than
a bee's sting!

Color the tarantula.

Find the spider that is different.

All birds have **feathers.**

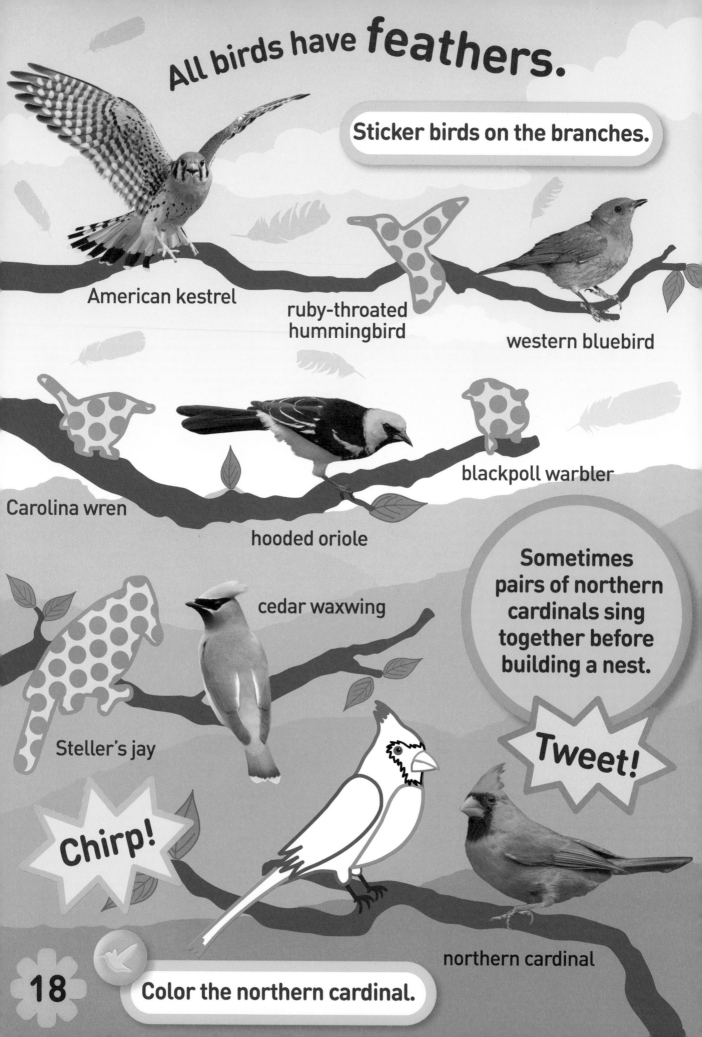

Sticker birds on the branches.

American kestrel

ruby-throated hummingbird

western bluebird

Carolina wren

hooded oriole

blackpoll warbler

cedar waxwing

Sometimes pairs of northern cardinals sing together before building a nest.

Steller's jay

Tweet!

Chirp!

northern cardinal

18

Color the northern cardinal.

The bald eagle can make a nest big enough to fit five six-year-old kids inside!

Follow the trails to find out which bird lives in the birdhouse.

tufted titmouse

blue jay

northern cardinal

HOME TWEET HOME

Rabbits and hares have **long ears!**

hare

Hares are bigger than rabbits and they have longer ears.

Help the hare hop through the maze to get to the vegetables.

Start

Finish

How many carrots can you count?

Stickers for pages 2 and 3

Stickers for pages 4 and 5

Extra stickers

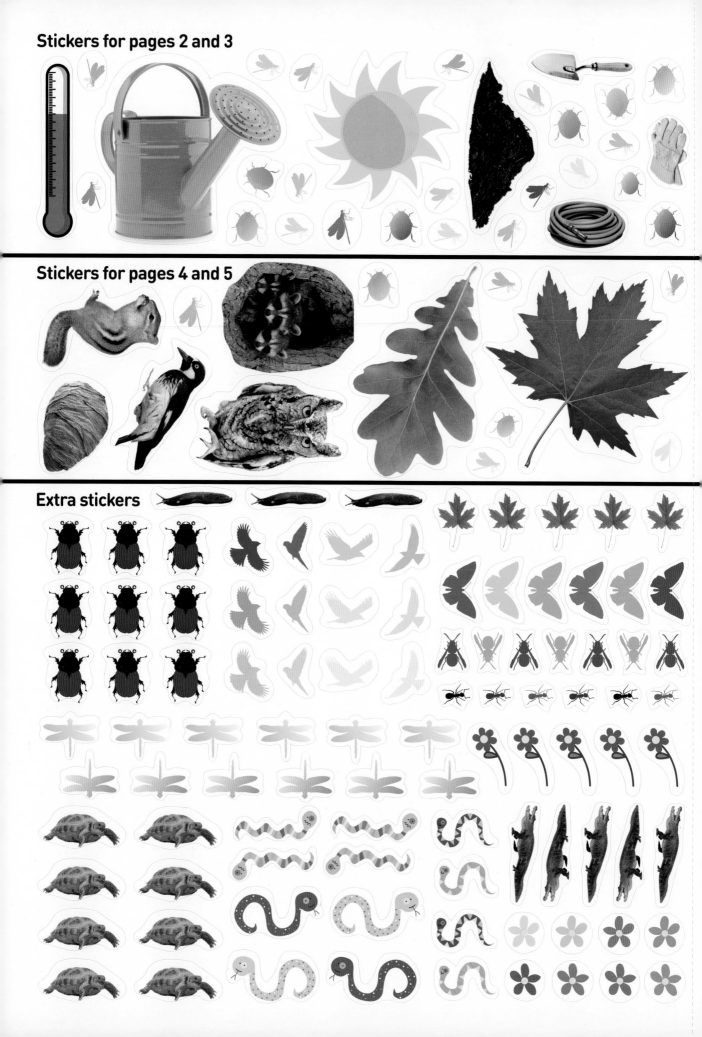

Stickers for pages 6 and 7

Stickers for pages 8 and 9

Extra stickers

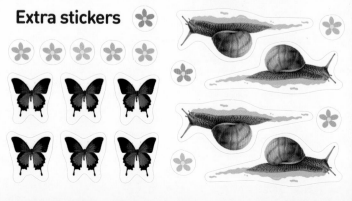

Stickers for pages 10 and 11

Stickers for pages 12 and 13

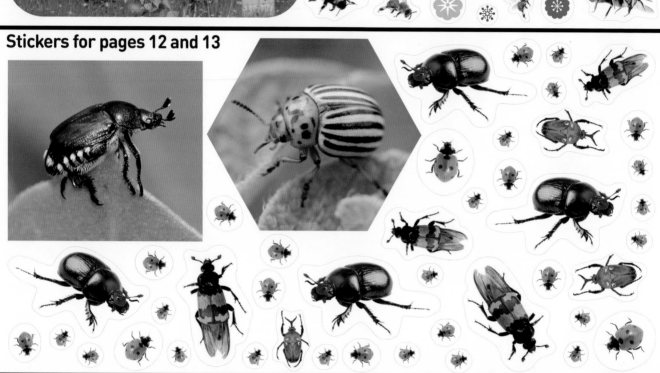

Extra stickers

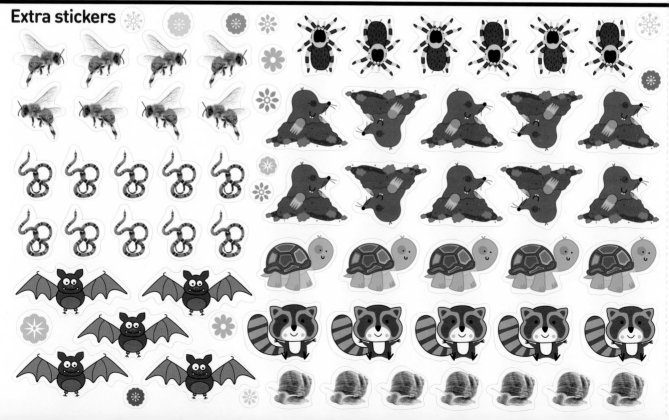

Stickers for pages 14 and 15

Stickers for pages 16 and 17

Stickers for pages 18 and 19

Extra stickers

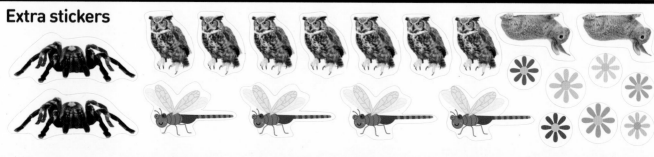

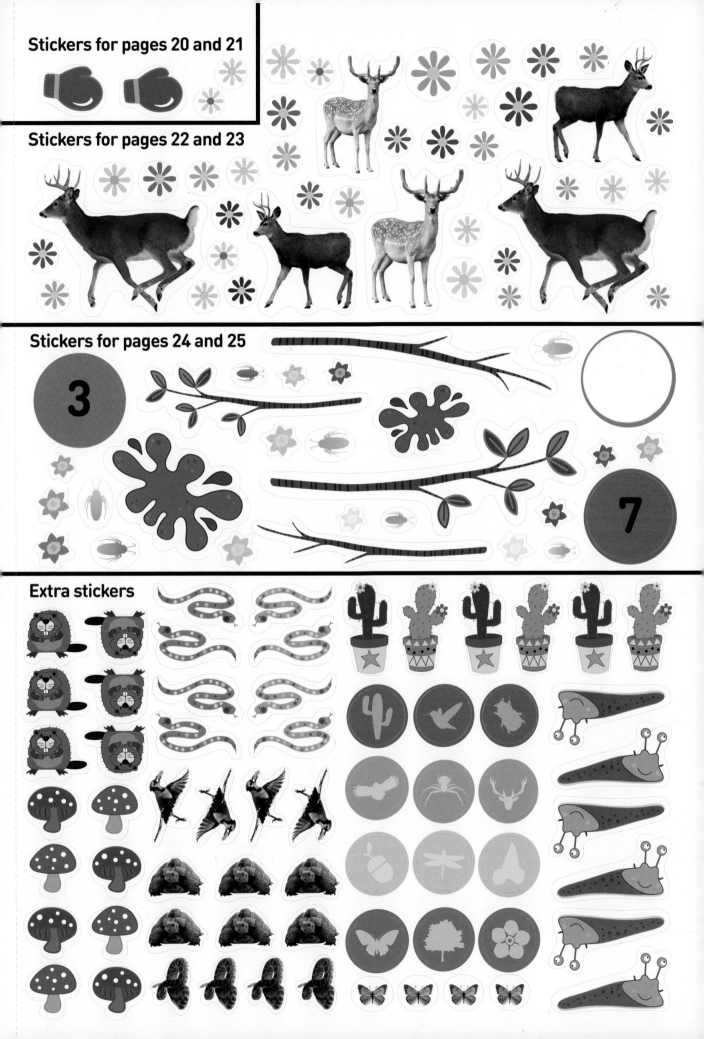

Stickers for pages 20 and 21

Stickers for pages 22 and 23

Stickers for pages 24 and 25

Extra stickers

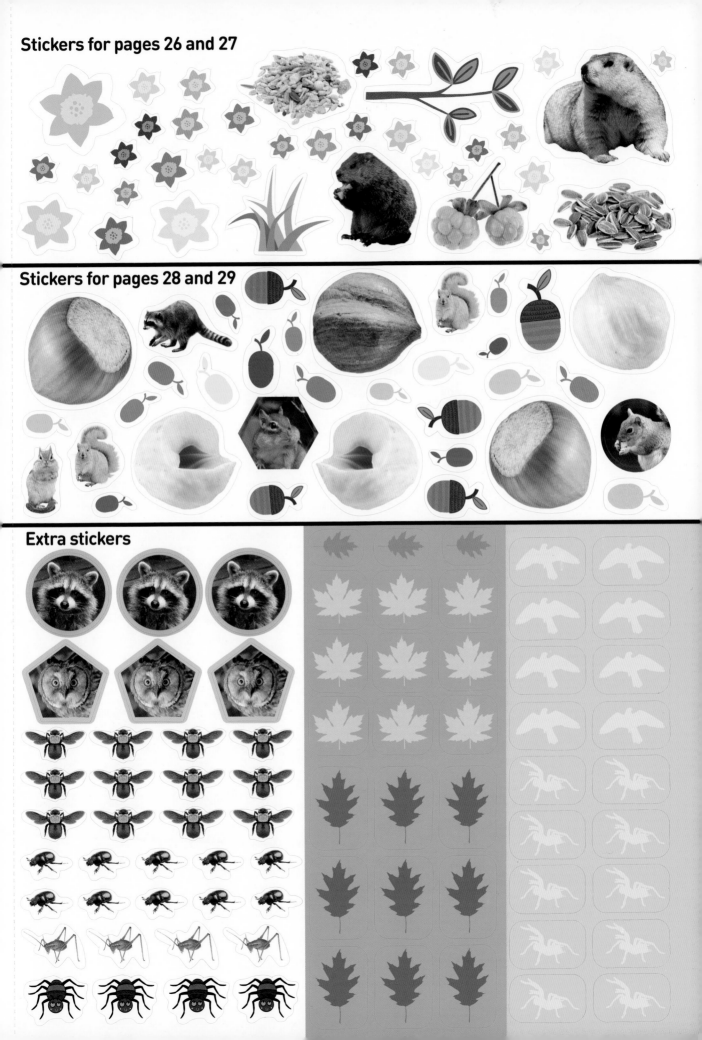

Stickers for pages 26 and 27

Stickers for pages 28 and 29

Extra stickers

Stickers for pages 30 and 31

Stickers for pages 32 and 33

Stickers for pages 34 and 35

Stickers for pages 36 and 37

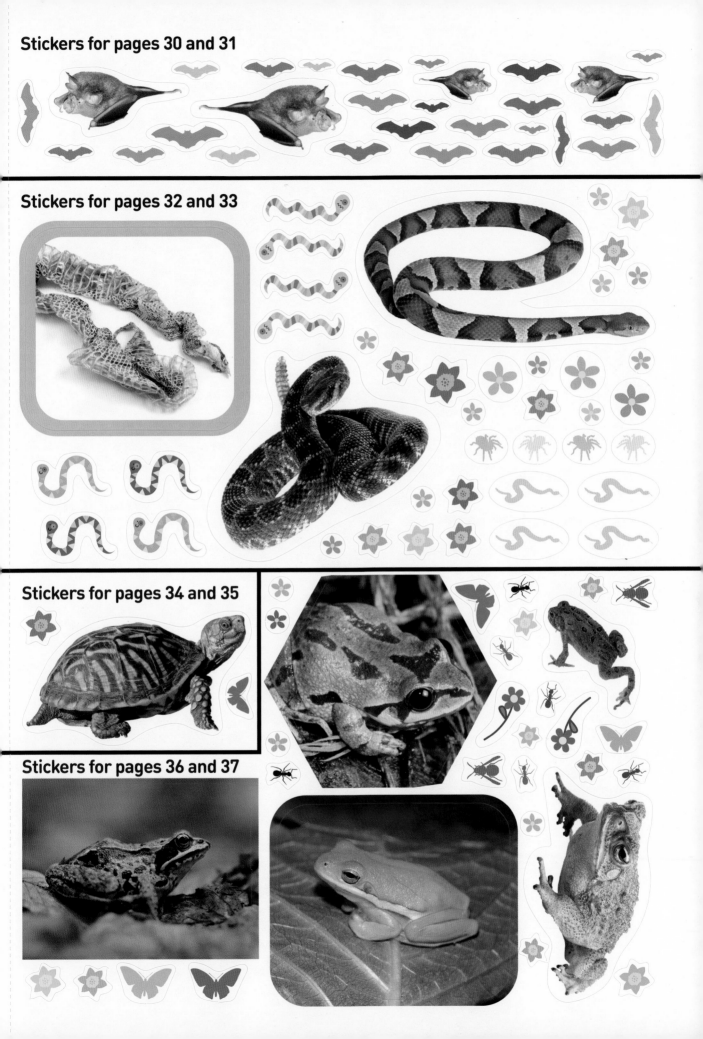

Stickers for pages 38 and 39

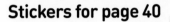

Stickers for page 40

Extra stickers

Follow the trails to find out which bunny lives in the burrow.

Hares can sometimes be seen boxing in springtime!

Sticker boxing gloves on the hares.

21

Some **deer** have **big** antlers!

Deer live together in big groups called herds.

Color the deer with a spotted pattern.

To attract females, male deer fight each other using their antlers.

elk

Sticker the deer in the correct boxes.

fallow deer

mule deer

whitetail deer

Look for four differences between the scenes.

23

Busy beavers make dams.

Beavers build dams in rivers or streams. Then they build their lodges behind their dams.

Sticker mud and sticks to finish the beavers' lodge.

24

Beavers' front teeth are always growing, but they are worn down by lots of gnawing on wood!

1 + 2 =

2 + 3 =

4 + 3 =

Beavers slap their tails on the water to warn each other of danger.

Color the beaver's tail.

25

Burrows make safe homes.

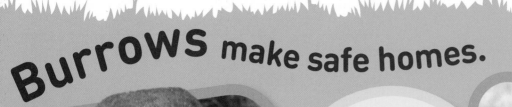

eastern mole

Moles, gophers, and woodchucks live in underground networks of burrows.

gopher

woodchuck

Help the mole through the burrow maze to find the worms.

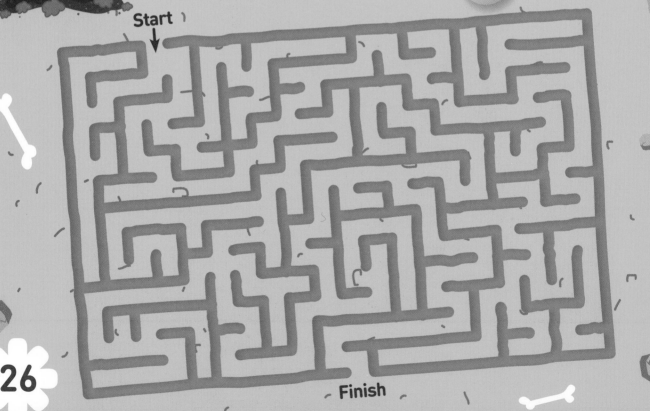

Start

Finish

Woodchucks can climb trees to get away from predators.

Sticker the woodchuck family. How many can you count?

Gophers carry food in their cheeks, which are called pockets!

Sticker more food!

Some animals are good **climbers!**

The black patches around a raccoon's eyes are called its eye mask.

Color the raccoon's mask and striped tail.

Chipmunks climb trees to find nuts.

Sticker more nuts for the hungry chipmunk.

Squirrels hide or bury nuts so they have enough food for winter.

fox squirrel

Fill the squirrel's store with acorns.

Find the missing stickers to finish the patterns.

29

Some animals come out after **dark.**

barn owl

saw-whet owl

Owls can twist and turn their heads almost all the way around to keep a lookout!

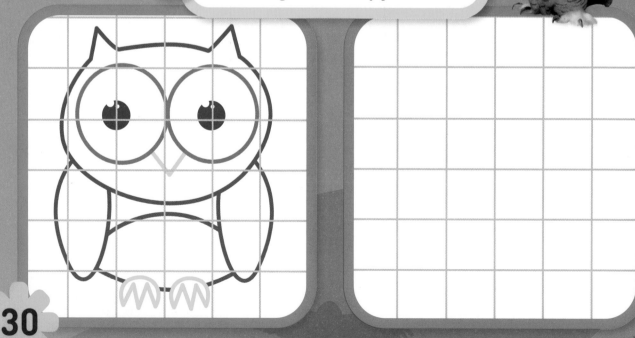

great gray owl

snowy owl

Use the grid to copy the owl.

30

Foxes can use their bushy tails like blankets to keep them warm in winter.

Color the fox.

little brown bat

dwarf fruit bat

A bat's wings are really thin flaps of skin between its long fingers.

Sticker more sleeping bats in the cave.

31

Slithering snakes hiss!

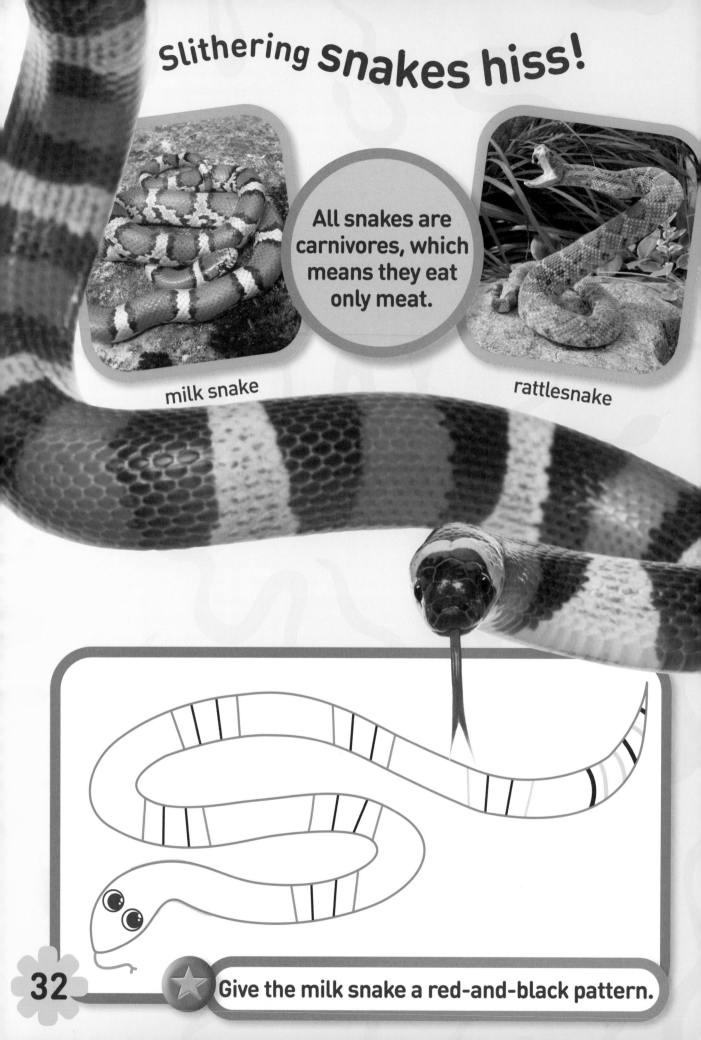

All snakes are carnivores, which means they eat only meat.

milk snake

rattlesnake

Give the milk snake a red-and-black pattern.

How many snakes can you count?

snakeskin

Sticker more snakes.

Snakes shed their skin as they grow bigger. They often leave whole skins behind!

Turtles and tortoises have **shells.**

Tortoises and turtles can live for a long time. The oldest turtle ever recorded was 188 years old!

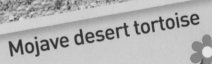

red-eared slider turtle

Mojave desert tortoise

Color the tortoise!

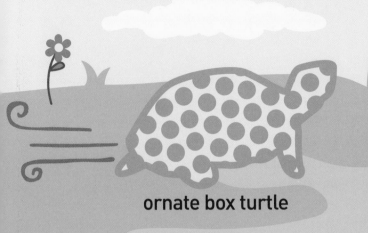

ornate box turtle

The fastest speed recorded for a tortoise was just 5 mph (8 km/h). That's about the same as your walking speed!

Follow the lines to find out which tortoise wins the race.

gopher tortoise

painted turtle

three-toed box turtle

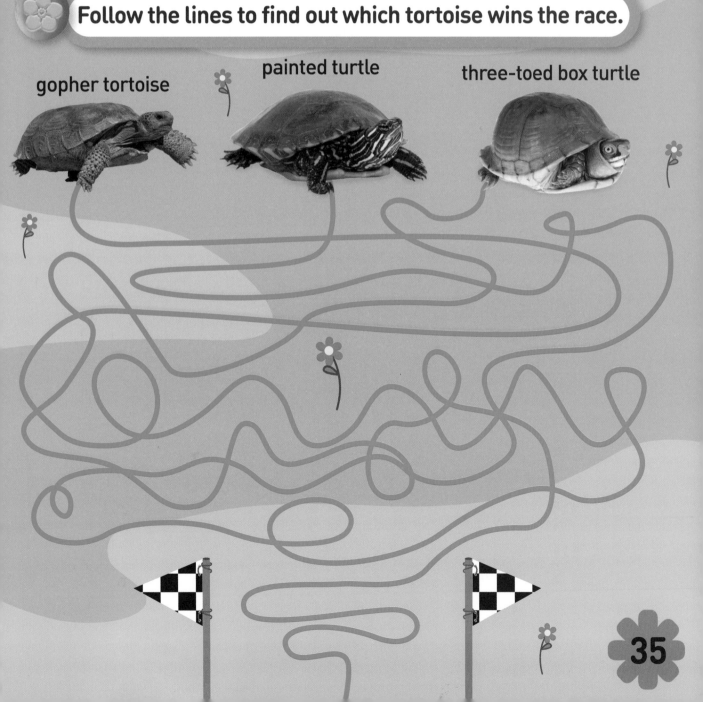

Frogs have **webbed** feet.

Ribbit!

Ribbit!

The American bullfrog gets its name from the sound it makes— its noise sounds like a bull!

Find the missing stickers!

American green tree frog

wood frog

Tadpoles are baby frogs.

chorus frog

northern leopard frog

Color the tadpoles.

36

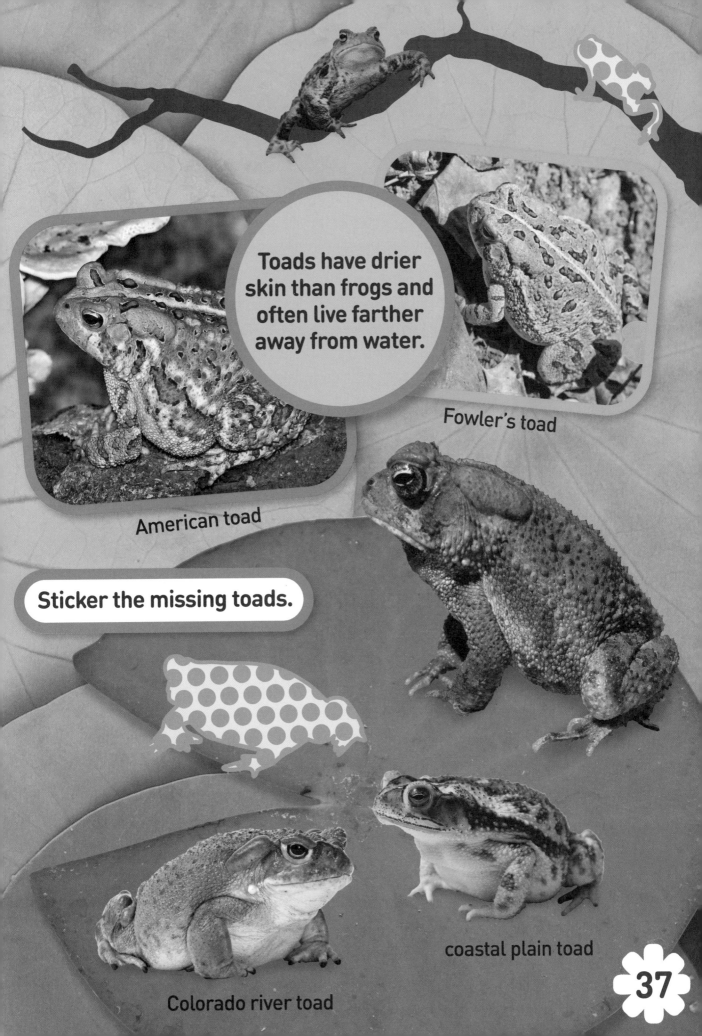

Toads have drier skin than frogs and often live farther away from water.

Fowler's toad

American toad

Sticker the missing toads.

Colorado river toad

coastal plain toad

37

Salamanders have slimy skin!

Salamanders will eat almost any creature they can swallow—including spiders, slugs, and worms!

Follow the lines to see what the salamander eats.

If a salamander loses a leg, it can grow a new one!

Newts are a type of salamander.

How many of each newt can you see hiding around the pond?

eastern newt ⬭

rough-skinned newt ⬭

California newt ⬭

39

My favorite backyard animals!

Find the missing stickers.

monarch butterfly

blue jay

rabbit

chipmunk

bald eagle

Draw your favorite animal.

Foreword

Shalom! For almost 2,000 years, the synagogue, like the home, has been the center of Jewish life.

Three Hebrew names for "synagogue" describe what goes on in it. We call the synagogue *Beit Tefilah*, a house of prayer. Here people gather to worship, sing praise to God, offer thanks, and ask for help. Wherever Jews gather together, there is a community of prayer. We don't need a special building to pray; we just need each other. Still, Jews have always constructed places to bring people together for prayer.

We call the synagogue *Beit Midrash*, a house of study. In every sanctuary is a book, the Torah. Jews are called the People of the Book. You will often find libraries in synagogues, and you will always find people, young and old, learning.

We call the synagogue *Beit Keneset*, a house of gathering. Actually, the word "synagogue" comes from two Greek words meaning "bringing together." It is where people come during good times and sad times. They mark important moments in life with each other. They come to do good deeds to help others.

In the synagogue you will see people welcome a new child into the community. Here young boys and girls of thirteen become bar and bat mitzvah, accepting their responsibilities to the Jewish people. Often weddings take place in the synagogue as the bride and groom stand under a *chuppah*, a wedding canopy. People also come to remember those they love who have died.

There are many symbols you will see in the synagogue. They help remind us about God, about Torah, and about living a good life. The information you find in this book will help you feel welcome. Come in!

Rabbi Sandy Eisenberg Sasso, D.Min.,
author of *God's Paintbrush, In God's Name,* and
Adam & Eve's First Sunset: God's New Day

Books in the Series

What You Will See Inside…

- *A Synagogue*

- *A Mosque*

- *A Catholic Church*

- *Lo que se puede ver dentro de una iglesia católica*

- *A Hindu Temple*

What You Will See Inside
A SYNAGOGUE

Rabbi Lawrence A. Hoffman
and Dr. Ron Wolfson
with Photographs by Bill Aron

NOVALIS

Walking Together, Finding the Way
SKYLIGHT PATHS Publishing
Woodstock, Vermont

For People of All Faiths, All Backgrounds
JEWISH LIGHTS Publishing
Woodstock, Vermont

What You Will See Inside a Synagogue

2004 First Printing
Text © 2004 Lawrence A. Hoffman and Ron Wolfson

For information regarding permission to reprint material from this book, please mail or fax your request in writing to SkyLight Paths Publishing, Permissions Department, at the address / fax number listed below, or e-mail your request to permissions@skylightpaths.com.

Library of Congress Cataloging-in-Publication Data
Hoffman, Lawrence A., 1942–
What you will see inside a synagogue / Lawrence Hoffman and Ron Wolfson.
p. cm. — (What you will see inside—)
ISBN 1-59473-012-1 (hardcover)
1. Judaism—Liturgy—Juvenile literature. 2. Judaism—Customs and practices—Juvenile literature. 3. Fasts and feasts—Judaism—Juvenile literature. 4. Synagogues—Juvenile literature. I. Wolfson, Ron. II. Title. III. Series.
BM660.H635 2004
296.4'6—dc22

2004011178

A catalogue record for this book is available from the National Library of Canada.
ISBN 2-89507-412-7

Grateful acknowledgment is given for permission to reprint images from the following sources: Bill Aron—page 3, page 5, page 6 *(Kippah),* page 7, page 8, page 9, page 10 *(Amidah),* page 11, page 12, page 13, page 14 *(Oneg Shabbat),* page 15, page 16, page 17 *(Seder Plate),* page 19, page 20 (bar mitzvah), page 21 *(Mazal Tov),* page 22, page 23, page 24, page 25, page 26, page 27, page 28, page 29, page 30; Richard S. Vosko—page 6 (Lobby, Congregation Immanuel, Denver, Colorado), page 31; Temple Beth-El Zedeck, Indianapolis—page 17 (boy in library), page 18 (soup kitchen); Jules Porter—page 20 (bat mitzvah); Joellyn Wallen Zollman—page 21 *(Chuppah);* Jonathan Kremer—page 21 *(K'tubah);* CCAR Press—page 10 *(Siddur).* Thanks to the following people for providing the photographs on page 4: Corinne Lightweaver (photograph by Stacey B. Peyer), Stuart M. Matlins, Rabbi Angela Warnick Buchdahl (photograph by George Kalinsky), Bill Aron, Rabbi Gershom Sizomu, Sylvia Boorstein, Aaron Bousel, Lauren Seidman (photograph by Michael H. Seidman), Zalman M. Schachter-Shalomi, Ron Wolfson.

10 9 8 7 6 5 4 3 2 1

Manufactured in China

> SkyLight Paths Publishing is creating a place where people of different spiritual traditions come together for challenge and inspiration, a place where we can help each other understand the mystery that lies at the heart of our existence.
>
> SkyLight Paths sees both believers and seekers as a community that increasingly transcends traditional boundaries of religion and denomination—people wanting to learn from each other, *walking together, finding the way.*

Book and Jacket Design: Dawn DeVries Sokol with Bridgett Taylor and Tim Holtz

SkyLight Paths, "Walking Together, Finding the Way" and colophon are trademarks of LongHill Partners, Inc., registered in the U.S. Patent and Trademark Office.

Walking Together, Finding the Way
Published by SkyLight Paths Publishing
A Division of LongHill Partners, Inc.
Sunset Farm Offices, Route 4, P.O. Box 237
Woodstock, VT 05091
Tel: (802) 457-4000   Fax: (802) 457-4004
www.skylightpaths.com

For People of All Faiths, All Backgrounds
Jewish Lights Publishing
A Division of LongHill Partners, Inc.
Sunset Farm Offices, Route 4, P.O. Box 237
Woodstock, VT 05091
Tel: (802) 457-4000   Fax: (802) 457-4004
www.jewishlights.com

Published in Canada by Novalis, Saint Paul University, Ottawa, Canada
Business Office:
Novalis
49 Front Street East, 2nd Floor
Toronto, Ontario, Canada
M5E 1B3
Phone: 1-877-702-7773 or (416) 363-3303
Fax: 1-877-702-7775 or (416) 363-9409
E-mail: cservice@novalis.ca
www.novalis.ca

Shalom! Welcome!

"*SHALOM!*"* is a greeting in Hebrew, a holy language for Jews. This book gives you some other Hebrew words for things that you may hear in synagogues. When you see this mark (*), look at the bottom of the page to see how the Hebrew word is pronounced.

Sometimes a synagogue is called a temple, or a *shul*,* a word that reminds us of "school," because synagogues are places for learning, not just praying. Learning is a very important part of Judaism.

Synagogues may be big or small, fancy or plain. No matter what they look like, however, all synagogues are places for learning, praying, and gathering together. People gather to celebrate happy times, to find comfort when they are sad, to give charity, and to do good deeds. In this book we focus mainly on the synagogues and services of the Conservative, Reconstructionist, and Reform movements in Judaism, the synagogues that you will see most in North America.

Everyone is welcome here, because Jews believe that every single person is made in God's image. That means that our goodness, our conscience, and our right to be treated with dignity make us like God. Synagogues are holy places, where everyone is welcome because everyone is holy—like God.

The most important room in a synagogue is its sanctuary, where we meet to pray. Mostly, this book shows you what is in the sanctuary. But sanctuaries are not just for things. They need people. So synagogues are for people. The Bible says, "May those who enter be blessed." When you enter a synagogue, we pray that God blesses you.

Welcome to the synagogue!

Shalom: shah-LOHM
Shul: SHOOL

Who Are the Jewish People?

JUDAISM IS A RELIGION, not a race or nationality. There are Jews of many different colors and from many different nations. What binds them together as a people are a shared way of living, beliefs, and rituals.

Gathering for Shabbat

ON WEEKDAYS, THE SYNAGOGUE FILLS WITH PEOPLE attending classes, looking for help, and working on projects. In some synagogues, people come every morning and evening to pray.

On the Sabbath—we call it by its Hebrew name, Shabbat*—and on Jewish holidays, even more people come to pray. When we enter, we stop to talk and greet one another with *Shabbat shalom** ("Have a peaceful Sabbath"), *Chag samei'ach!** ("Happy holiday"), or *Shanah tovah** ("Have a good new year"), depending on the occasion. As people come in, someone who is part of the congregation may welcome them, whether they are Jewish or not, and especially if they have never visited before. Judaism encourages us to welcome strangers.

On the right-hand doorpost of every synagogue is a small decorative container called a *m'zuzah**. It reminds us that this is God's house. People who enter and leave the building may touch the *m'zuzah* with their finger-tips, and then put their fingers to their lips as if offering a kiss, as a sign of respect for God. Each special room in the synagogue (the sanctuary, the classrooms, and the library, for example) may have its own *m'zuzah*.

Jewish homes also have a *m'zuzah*, to remind us that our homes should be filled with love and kindness. A synagogue is like a big Jewish home for all Jews—and for anyone else who wants to visit.

M'ZUZAH: The *m'zuzah* tells us, "This is a holy place." God visits us in our homes, and we visit God in the synagogue.

Shabbat: shah-BAHT
Shabbat shalom: shah-BAHT shah-LOHM
Chag samei'ach: KHAG sah-MAY-akh
Shanah tovah: shah-NAH toh-VAH, or SHAH-nah TOH-vah
M'zuzah: m'-zoo-ZAH, or m'-ZOO-zah
Sh'ma: sh'-MAH

SH'MA: Inside the *m'zuzah* is a handwritten prayer called the *Sh'ma**, a section of the Bible that reminds us to love God, just as God loves us. The main words of the *Sh'ma* are, "Hear O Israel, the Eternal is our God, the Eternal alone."

KIPPAH: Some men and women wear a *kippah*— a special head covering— in the synagogue to show respect for God, and some people wear them all the time.

Preparing for Prayer

TALLIT: Some people wrap themselves in their *tallit*, when they first put it on, to help them concentrate on being with God.

IN SOME SYNAGOGUES, people wear a special head covering, a *kippah**, and a prayer shawl, a *tallit**. The *kippah* is also called a *yarmulke**. Wearing it shows respect for God. The *tallit* comes in many sizes and colors, but it always contains four long knotted fringes (called *tsitsit**) on each corner. Long ago, the Bible says, God rescued Jews from slavery in Egypt. Some people say when Jews look at the fringes, they remember how bad it is to be a slave, and how important it is to treat everyone kindly and with respect.

The *tsitsit* are arranged so that they add up to the number of *mitzvot**, or commandments, God has told us to do. When we look at the *tsitsit*, we are reminded to do what God asks of us.

In some synagogues (called Orthodox), the *kippah* and *tallit* are usually worn only by men. In other synagogues (called Reform, Conservative, and Reconstructionist), women frequently wear them too.

The people you see here have just arrived and are getting ready to enter the sanctuary, which is through the open doorway. Each is getting a prayer book, called a *siddur**. Then they might put on a *tallit*. Some people wear a *kippah* all the time, not just in the synagogue, because God is everywhere.

Kippah: kee-PAH
Tallit: tah-LEET
Yarmulke: YAHR-mul-kuh
Tsitsit: tsee-TSEET
Mitzvot: meets-VOHT
Siddur: see-DOOR, or SIH-d'r
T'fillin: t'FILL-in

T'FILLIN: At prayer services in the morning, some people wear *t'fillin**, small boxes that are placed on the forehead (next to the brain) and on the inside of the upper arm (next to the heart)—the places where we think and feel. The boxes are held in place by leather straps, tied in the shape of the Hebrew letters that spell God's name. Like the *m'zuzah*, the boxes hold the prayer we call the *Sh'ma*.

TSITSIT: Specially knotted fringes on the four corners of the *tallit* also remind us of the "four corners of the earth" where all God's people live.

INSIDE THE ARK: When the ark is opened, you can see the many Torah scrolls standing beside one another, each dressed in a special covering and decorated with silver crowns and plates.

The Holiest Place in the Synagogue

FOR JEWS, THE HOLIEST BOOK IN THE WORLD is the Hebrew Bible. The holiest part of the Hebrew Bible is its first part, the five books of Moses, which we call the Torah. It tells the story of how our ancestors first met God and found out how God wants us to live.

The Torah is handwritten in beautifully decorated Hebrew letters on a material called parchment, which is rolled up into a scroll. The Torah scrolls are kept in an ark, a cabinet at the front of the sanctuary. The ark is the holiest place in the synagogue. It usually holds many Torah scrolls. Jews treat Torah scrolls so carefully and with such respect that they can be used over and over again for hundreds of years.

BIMAH: The area where the people who lead the prayers stand. In some synagogues, the *bimah* is in the middle of the sanctuary instead of at the front.

Above the ark is a *ner tamid**, an "eternal light" that shines day and night to symbolize God's presence. The ark is usually on the eastern wall, so that during prayer, Jews can face the ark and Jerusalem, the city that Jews consider the holiest place on earth.

In front of the ark is the *bimah**. It is the raised platform where the people who lead prayers usually stand. Sometimes it has a candle-holder called a *m'norah**. The one you see in the picture holds seven candles, just like the *m'norah* that the Israelites of the Bible made. The *bimah* may have other things, too, like an eight-branched *m'norah* that is used on the holiday of Chanukah and is sometimes called a *chanukiyah**; a six-pointed Jewish star, called *magen david**, the "star of David," named after King David of the Bible; or decorations shaped like a lion, called Lion of Judah, the sign for a biblical tribe (where the name "Judaism" comes from). Look also for flags of the country where you live, and of Israel, the Jewish "homeland," where most of the Bible stories happened.

SHABBAT CANDLES: In Judaism, each new day begins at sundown and continues through the next morning and afternoon. Saturday is a holy day—the Sabbath, called Shabbat. On Friday night, when it begins, you may see someone on the *bimah* lighting two Shabbat candles to bring the light of Shabbat joy to people.

Ner tamid: NAYR tah-MEED   *M'norah:* m'NOH-rah, or m'-noh-RAH   *Magen david:* mah-GAYN dah-VEED
Bimah: BEE-mah   *Chanukiyah:* khah-noo-ki-YAH

How Jews Pray

JEWS PRAY DIRECTLY TO GOD, but our prayers are usually led by two people: a cantor (called *chazan** in Hebrew) and a rabbi. They are called messengers of the congregation because they help direct our prayers to God. The cantor sings or chants melodies that reflect the mood of the service. The rabbi reads the prayers aloud, and teaches about Judaism by giving a sermon during the service. All Jews are encouraged to learn how to lead prayers, however, and anyone can become a rabbi or cantor. The Hebrew word *rabbi* means "teacher."

Do you remember the name of the prayer book? It is called a *siddur*, which means "order." The prayer service has an order to it and is often read in Hebrew, the ancient language of the Bible.

During a service, we usually sit, but we sometimes stand, especially during a prayer called the *Amidah**, when people may pray silently or in a whisper, as if personally "standing before God."

In some synagogues, musical instruments are played.

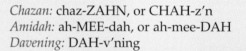

Chazan: chaz-ZAHN, or CHAH-z'n
Amidah: ah-MEE-dah, or ah-mee-DAH
Davening: DAH-v'ning

These are duties whose worth cannot be measured:
honoring one's father and mother,
acts of love and kindness,
diligent pursuit of knowledge and wisdom,
hospitality to strangers,
visiting the sick,
celebrating with bride and groom,
consoling the bereaved,
praying with sincerity,
and making peace where there is strife.
And the study of Torah leads to them all.

אֵלוּ דְבָרִים שֶׁאֵין לָהֶם שִׁעוּר:
כִּבּוּד אָב וָאֵם,
וּגְמִילוּת חֲסָדִים,
וְהַשְׁכָּמַת בֵּית הַמִּדְרָשׁ
שַׁחֲרִית וְעַרְבִית,
וְהַכְנָסַת אוֹרְחִים,
וּבִקוּר חוֹלִים,
וְהַכְנָסַת כַּלָּה,
וּלְוָיַת הַמֵּת,
וְעִיּוּן תְּפִלָּה,
וַהֲבָאַת שָׁלוֹם בֵּין אָדָם
לַחֲבֵרוֹ.
וְתַלְמוּד תּוֹרָה כְּנֶגֶד כֻּלָּם.

SIDDUR: This *siddur* is open at a prayer that people say together. In this prayer book, Hebrew and English appear on both pages, and people pray mostly in English. Sometimes people pray entirely in Hebrew.

AMIDAH: The whole congregation stands to say the *Amidah* (the "standing prayer"). Sometimes the cantor sings part of it out loud. Often the people join in, as they do with many parts of the service that are sung. In some synagogues, the people read a prayer by *davening** it—that is, they all read it aloud, but by themselves, not all together. It sounds like mumbling, but really they are praying to God at their own speed, starting all together and then waiting until everyone finishes, before the cantor sings the last few lines and everyone begins again at the next paragraph.

Reading the Torah

ON SHABBAT AND HOLIDAYS—and on Mondays and Thursdays, too—someone reads part of the Torah scroll out loud. Each week, a different part is read; then the Torah is rolled forward for the next week, until, at the end of a year, we read the last little bit and then roll it back to the beginning and start all over again.

Whenever we read Torah, we remove it from the ark with great respect, and parade through the congregation holding it. The tiny bells that are part of its covering jingle as the parade moves through the synagogue. People crowd into the aisles to get close enough to the scroll to kiss it by touching it with the fringes of the *tallit* (the *tsitsit*), a prayer book, or even their fingers. Then they kiss whatever they used to touch it, to show their love for Torah. The Torah is then placed upon a special reading table, sometimes in the middle of the congregation, where its cover and ornaments are removed, so that someone can read from it.

YAD: As a sign of respect for the Torah, and to make sure the letters aren't blurred by touching them with fingers, the Torah reader keeps place with a pointer shaped like a human hand at the end. It is called a *yad**, the Hebrew word for "hand."

People from the congregation take turns standing beside the person reading Torah. They say prayers to thank God for giving us the Torah on Mount Sinai. This is called an *aliyah**. When the reading is finished, someone holds the Torah up high so everyone can see its writing, and someone else puts the Torah covering and decorations back on. Sometimes, the Torah is then paraded once again through the congregation before being put back in the ark.

Aliyah: ah-LEE-yah, or ah-lee-YAH
Yad: YAHD
Hakafah: hah-kah-FAH
Simchat Torah: sim-KHAT toh-RAH

HAKAFAH: The parade through the congregation is called a *hakafah**. At an autumn holiday called Simchat Torah*, we finish reading the Torah and then begin it all over again. The Torah parade that day is especially joyous. Children wave flags, and people lead the way dancing around the room, while carrying the Torah.

TORAH SCROLL: Before the Torah is put back in the ark, someone shows the congregation its beautiful writing. It is handwritten by someone specially trained to make every letter perfectly. Many of the letters are decorated.

Enjoying Shabbat

AT THE CONCLUSION OF THE SHABBAT SERVICE IN THE SANCTUARY, everyone is invited to another room to celebrate together at the *Oneg Shabbat**. *Oneg* means "joy." *Oneg Shabbat* means "enjoying Shabbat."

The *Oneg Shabbat* starts with the *Kiddush**, a prayer over wine or grape juice, followed by a blessing over a bread called a *challah**. If it is a Friday evening service, the *Oneg Shabbat* will probably have a large dessert table. Saturday morning prayer services are usually followed with lunch or just a snack. Some people call it a *kiddush*, after the name of the prayer with which it begins.

Jews believe that God wants us to do certain things called "commandments," not just the Ten Commandments, but many more. Each one is called a mitzvah*. All together, they are called *mitzvot*. It is a mitzvah to attend synagogue prayer services on Shabbat and holidays. It is also a mitzvah to eat together afterward. Mitzvah has also come to mean "good deed."

Oneg Shabbat: OH-neg shah-BAHT
Kiddush: kee-DOOSH, or KIH-dish
Challah: KHAH-lah, or khah-LAH
Mitzvah: meets-VAH, or MITS-vah

KIDDUSH CUP: Over the centuries, Jews have made beautiful wine cups, usually of silver, and used them to celebrate holy days like Shabbat. Some synagogues have small museums or showcases with *kiddush* cups and other things that you see in this book.

SHARING THE *CHALLAH:* Sometimes people simply cut the *challah* in slices before eating it, but the people here are having fun as they get ready to tear off a piece for each person.

***CHALLAH* PLATE:** This special plate is decorated with Hebrew letters.

***CHALLAH* COVER:** The *challah* on this plate has a decorated cover. This one says (in Hebrew) "Jerusalem."

TALMUD: The Talmud has more than a thousand pages just like this one. The main reading is in the middle of the page. Comments by readers who lived hundreds of years ago are printed all around the borders. People study the center first, and then read the comments around the page. Some Jews try to study a different page every day. Others study just one page for many days. Studying Talmud is for advanced students; it is like going to "Jewish college."

Prayer and Learning Go Together

WE SOMETIMES PRAY NOT JUST IN THE SANCTUARY, but in other rooms too—especially the synagogue library, where this boy is standing. He may have just finished praying there with the adults and other children. If so, a Torah scroll was probably moved there so it could be read during the prayers.

Because the synagogue is a place of Jewish learning—not just prayer—the synagogue library, which has many books about Judaism, is a very important place. Some people spend Shabbat afternoon taking a class there—in the Bible, perhaps, or the Talmud,* a big set of books on almost every Jewish subject, written more than a thousand years ago, and almost as holy to us as our Bible.

People can pray in the library, but also study in the sanctuary. The synagogue also has classrooms where everyone (not just children) can learn about Judaism. They know that in Judaism, learning is as important as prayer.

Talmud: TAHL-m'd
Pesach: PEH-sakh
Seder: SAY-d'r

SEDER PLATE: Most synagogues have a gift shop where people can buy ritual objects for their home. We use this plate on the holiday of Passover, or Pesach*. Passover celebrates the time long ago when God freed our ancestors from slavery in Egypt. The seder plate holds special kinds of food that we use for a Passover dinner called a Seder*. If you are invited to a Seder, look for the special foods there, and ask someone to explain them to you.

Fixing the World

A JEWISH STORY SAYS THAT when God created the world, something went wrong. God sent light throughout the universe, but it got mixed with darkness. Ever since then, we try to rescue the light from the darkness. We call that *tikkun olam**, "fixing the world." We fix the world by doing good deeds, like preparing food for a soup kitchen. We go to synagogues not just for ourselves, but to help others. Some synagogues even open up at night to let homeless people stay there.

Synagogues are like repair shops for the people in our world who are broken. We say that all human beings are partners with God in creation. God started creation, but we have to finish it by fixing God's world.

Tikkun olam: tee-KOON oh-LAHM
Tzedakah: ts'-dah-KAH, or ts'-DAH-kah

TZEDAKAH: Jews are supposed to give charity every day, so after prayer, everyone may contribute money for good causes. It may be collected in a *tzedakah** box like this one. *Tzedakah* means "doing the right thing." By giving money to those in need, we help fix the world.

Bar and Bat Mitzvah ...

JEWS GO TO THE SYNAGOGUE to celebrate important times in their lives. At about the thirteenth birthday, a boy becomes a bar mitzvah and a girl becomes a bat mitzvah.

At their bar or bat mitzvah ceremony, we recognize that they are becoming independent teenagers. They are not yet fully grown up, but starting then, they can practice being adults, because they are old enough to be responsible for what they do. When they come to the synagogue on their bar or bat mitzvah day, they are treated like adults. They will already have studied how to lead Jewish lives, and learned how to read Hebrew, so that when they become a

bar mitzvah or a bat mitzvah, they are allowed (for the very first time) to lead the congregation in prayer— the way the rabbi and cantor usually do. The best moment comes when they read the Torah themselves, and the rabbi asks God to bless them.

Family and friends come from all over to witness the ceremony and participate in this passing along of Jewish tradition. The boys and girls are now ready to join the synagogue youth group. If they continue their Jewish studies, they may graduate in a synagogue ceremony called confirmation.

... And Weddings, Too

Jews have everyday names, and special Hebrew names as well. Children do not remember it, but as babies, they were probably given Hebrew names at a ceremony in a synagogue. When they're grown up, they may get married in a synagogue, too.

A Jewish wedding often takes place in the synagogue sanctuary, under a canopy called a *chuppah**. The *chuppah* represents the new home that the bride and groom will make together. It is open on all sides to show that their home will be open to guests, and even to strangers, whom they will welcome.

Chuppah: khoo-PAH, or KHUH-pah
Mazal tov: MAH-z'l TOV
K'tubah: k'-TOO-bah

CHUPPAH: The Jewish wedding canopy represents the new home that the bride and groom will make together.

MAZAL TOV: The wedding ends by the groom stamping on a glass so that it shatters. Even in this moment of their own great happiness, the couple knows that other people in the world are sick and suffering—broken, like the glass—and needing help that the bride and groom promise to give them. When the glass breaks, everyone in the room shouts *"Mazal tov*,"* the Hebrew way of saying, "Congratulations!"

K'TUBAH: The bride and groom have had a *k'tubah**, a specially designed marriage certificate, made for them. This one is decorated with images of Jerusalem.

Celebrating Holidays

WE CELEBRATE JEWISH HOLIDAYS at home and in the synagogue. Chanukah* lasts eight days and is a lot of fun, because we play games with a spinning top called a *dreidel**, and we eat special foods like potato pancakes called *latkes** and doughnuts called *sufganiyot**. People give each other Chanukah presents and say "Happy Chanukah!"

The most important moment comes every evening, when we say prayers, sing songs, and light candles on the special Chanukah *m'norah* that some Jews call a *chanukiyah*. On the first night, we light one candle, using another candle called the *shamash** to light it. Each night, we add a candle, until, by the last night, all eight candles (and the *shamash,* which makes nine) shine brightly. We put the *m'norah* in the window, and light up the darkness outside.

PURIM: Like Chanukah, Purim* too is a holiday for fun. Many people, especially children, come to the synagogue in costume to remember a time when the Jews of Persia escaped a terrible danger. We read the *m'gillah**, a scroll that tells the biblical story of a brave Jewish woman named Esther. Esther saved her people from Haman, an evil man who wanted to kill all the Jews. When the name "Haman" is read aloud, everyone boos and makes noise with a special noise-maker called a *gragger**. Can you imagine booing in a sanctuary!?

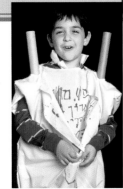

GRAGGER: A *gragger* is used to make noise during the Purim story.

Chanukah is celebrated to remember how God saved the Jewish People from an evil king, long ago. The bright lights remind everyone that God helps us in times of darkness.

Chanukah: KHAH-noo-kah
Dreidel: DRAY-d'l
Latkes: LOT-kes
Sufganiyot: soof-gah-ni-YOHT
Shamash: shah-MAHSH
Gelt: GEHLT
Purim: POO-rim, or poo-REEM
M'gillah: m'GIH-lah, or m'gee-LAH
Gragger: GRAH-g'r

CHANUKIYAH: A *m'norah* with nine candles used to celebrate Chanukah.

DREIDELS: Fancy *dreidels* for Chanukah games. The *dreidel* is spun like a top, and you win or lose depending on which side lands upward. Prizes are often chocolates, sometimes wrapped in gold or silver foil to look like money, and called *gelt**.

The High Holy Days

DURING THE FALL, we celebrate two holidays called the High Holy Days. Almost all Jews come to synagogue for these joyous—but very serious—days of reflection. We think about our behavior in the past year, ask for forgiveness of God and each other, and promise to do better in the year ahead. The rabbi and the cantor wear white robes, and even the Torah scrolls are dressed in white, because white is a symbol of fresh starts. As symbols of their new beginning, some people buy new clothes to wear then.

First comes Rosh Hashanah*, the Jewish New Year. We pray for a blessed and successful year, and we blow a *shofar*, a ram's horn, as a "wake-up call" to remind us to try to be good people. Synagogue prayers often include a choir singing beautiful music. People wish each other *"Shanah tovah*—Have a good year." Some people add, "Have a good and *sweet* year." Happy New Year!

Yom Kippur*, the most holy day of the Jewish year, comes ten days later. It begins with a sundown service called *Kol Nidre*, named after the most important prayer of the evening. We go home to sleep but return the next morning for a whole day of prayer. In order to concentrate on our prayers for forgiveness, adults and teenagers fast all day. That means we do not eat or drink anything. Children too may try to fast for a while, if they wish to. When Yom Kippur ends, we return home from the synagogue to "break the fast" and enjoy a festive meal.

ROSH HASHANAH AND YOM KIPPUR PRAYERS: On Rosh Hashanah and Yom Kippur, people think about how they acted the past year, pray for forgiveness, and look forward to the year ahead.

ROSH HASHANAH APPLES AND HONEY: We eat apples dipped in honey, because we hope we will have a sweet year.

Rosh Hashanah: ROSH-hah-SHAH-nah, or ROSH hah-shah-NAH
Shofar: sho-FAR
Yom Kippur: yohm kee-POOR, or yohm KIH-p'r
Kol Nidre: KOHL need-RAY; or kohl NID-ray

BLOWING THE *SHOFAR*: This man has even his head wrapped in a big white *tallit.* You cannot see his face because he is facing away from you, so that he can look at the ark and the Torah scrolls while he blows the *shofar.*

Showing Our Thanks

FIVE DAYS AFTER YOM KIPPUR, we show our thanks to God in a harvest holiday called Sukkot*.

Long ago, our ancestors who were farmers built small huts in their fields during the harvest season. They stayed there day and night while gathering their crops. Today, we too build a temporary outdoor hut called a *sukkah**. It is decorated with tree branches, garden vegetables hung up on string, and, sometimes, the New Year greeting cards that we received for Rosh Hashanah.

After prayer services, we go to the *sukkah* for the *kiddush*. Even though people build a *sukkah* in their synagogue, many families build one at home, outdoors—in their yard, perhaps, or on the roof of their apartment building—so they can see the sky just the way the farmers long ago must have. Some people eat all their meals and even sleep in their *sukkah*.

Sukkot is a holiday of hospitality. "Pretend guests," like the great men and women of the Bible, are invited to visit. Real guests come to eat there also. If you are invited to a *sukkah*, you can bring something to hang up as part of the decoration.

During Sukkot prayer services, we use a *lulav** and an *etrog**. The *lulav* is a bundle of branches from trees that are mentioned in the Bible. They grow in Israel, but, depending on where you live, they might also grow in your backyard. The *etrog* is a fruit that looks like a lemon. People hold these objects together and wave them in all four directions, thanking God for making things grow all over the world.

Sukkot: soo-KOHT
Sukkah: soo-KAH, or SUH-kah
Lulav: LOO-lahv, or loo-LAHV
Etrog: ET-rohg, or et-ROHG

LULAV AND ETROG: The *lulav* is made of branches from trees mentioned in the Bible. We buy a new *lulav* and *etrog* every year, looking for the most beautiful ones we can find, to say, "Thank you, God, for giving us food."

MEMORIAL WALL: This synagogue has many plaques with the names of people who have died. On Yom Kippur, all the lights are lit.

How We Remember

REMEMBERING OUR PAST IS VERY IMPORTANT TO JEWS. On one of the walls of most synagogues, you will find rows of small metal signs. On them are shown the names of people in our families who have died. They are called memorial plaques. Often, there is a small light bulb next to the name, which is lighted on the anniversary of a person's death. That day, relatives of the person who died come to the synagogue to say a prayer called the *Kaddish** and to remember the person. On Yom Kippur, when the synagogue is packed with people, all the lights are lit. We also light *yahrtzeit** candles at home to remember people in our own family who have died. *Yahrtzeit* means the anniversary of the time when people we remember died.

YAHRTZEIT CANDLES: This *yahrtzeit* candle glows brightly all day and all night, even in the darkness, to remind us that people who we loved but who have died can still shine brightly in our memory.

In the synagogue, we remember good times and bad. There was a terrible time called the Holocaust. The Hebrew name for Holocaust is *Sho'ah**. It was a time when some evil people called the Nazis killed six million Jewish children, women, and men in Europe. A day of remembrance called Yom Hasho'ah* brings Jews to the synagogue to remember that terrible time.

But mostly, we remember good people and think about the times when they were still living. We also honor people who are still alive by remembering all the good things they have done. Some synagogues have pictures of the people who were their rabbis and leaders, and sometimes there are pictures of confirmation classes from the past.

Remember the young people becoming bar mitzvah and bat mitzvah? If they help the synagogue when they grow up, they may some day have their pictures on a wall of their synagogues.

Kaddish: KAH-dish, or kah-DEESH
Yahrtzeit: YAHR-tsite, or YOHR-tsite
Sh'oah: SHOH-ah
Yom Hasho'ah: YOM hah-SHOH-ah

ADAT SHALOM—LOS ANGELES, CALIFORNIA

TEMPLE BETH ISRAEL—BILOXI, MISSISSIPPI

ANSHE SFARD—NEW ORLEANS, LOUISIANA

L'hitra'ot. Come again.

THERE ARE MANY SYNAGOGUES ALL OVER THE WORLD. You can find one wherever Jews have lived—and that is just about everywhere! Synagogues are all different, but in many ways they are also the same. They are different because Jews live in different places and build synagogues that reflect their lives. They are the same because all synagogues are spiritual places for Jews—holy places for praying to God, studying the Torah, and doing good deeds.

The Hebrew word for "Goodbye" is *L'hitra'ot**. It means, "See you again!"

So: *L'hitra'ot!* Come again to visit us.

L'hitra'ot: l'-hit-rah-OHT

BETH ELOHIM—CHARLESTON, SOUTH CAROLINA

GATES OF THE GROVE SYNAGOGUE—EAST HAMPTON, NEW YORK

CENTRAL SYNAGOGUE—NEW YORK, NEW YORK